Ways to P
WE PLAY
SPORTS!

By Leonard Atlantic

Please visit our website, www.garethstevens.com. For a free color catalog of all our high-quality books, call toll free 1-800-542-2595 or fax 1-877-542-2596.

Cataloging-in-Publication Data

Names: Atlantic, Leonard.
Title: We play sports! / Leonard Atlantic.
Description: New York : Gareth Stevens Publishing, 2018. | Series: Ways to play | Includes index.
Identifiers: ISBN 9781482463538 (pbk.) | ISBN 9781482463552 (library bound) | ISBN 9781482463545 (6 pack)
Subjects: LCSH: Sports–Juvenile literature.
Classification: LCC GV705.4 A43 2018 | DDC 796–dc23

Published in 2018 by
Gareth Stevens Publishing
111 East 14th Street, Suite 349
New York, NY 10003

Copyright © 2018 Gareth Stevens Publishing

Editor: Ryan Nagelhout
Designer: Bethany Perl

Photo credits: Cover, p. 1 Rawpixel.com/Shutterstock.com; p. 5 holbox/Shutterstock.com; pp. 7, 11 Brocreative/Shutterstock.com; p. 9 matimix/Shutterstock.com; pp. 13, 15 Studio 1One/Shutterstock.com; p. 17, 19 Rob Hainer/Shutterstock.com; p. 21 Marcel Jancovic/Shutterstock.com; p. 23 AS photo studio/Shutterstock.com.

All rights reserved. No part of this book may be reproduced in any form without permission in writing from the publisher, except by a reviewer.

Printed in the United States of America

CPSIA compliance information: Batch #CS17GS: For further information contact Gareth Stevens, New York, New York at 1-800-542-2595.

Contents

Get Out and Play 4

Play at the Park 10

Football with Friends . . . 12

Baseball Brother 16

Words to Know 24

Index 24

My friends love to play.
They love sports!

My friend Jill has a soccer ball.

We love to kick it.

We play soccer at the park.

Dave loves
to play football.

We throw it
to each other.
This is called
playing catch!

My brother likes baseball.

He has his own glove.

I love to bowl.

I have my own ball.
It is pink!

Words to Know

bowling ball · football · glove

Index

baseball 16
football 12
glove 18
soccer 6, 10